The Tigers, They Let Me

☙

by Anis Mojgani

Write Bloody Publishing

writebloody.com

Copyright © Anis Mojgani, 2023.

All rights reserved. No part of this book may be used, performed, or reproduced in any manner whatsoever without written permission from the publisher except in the case of brief quotations embodied in critical articles or reviews.

First edition.
ISBN: 978-1949342512

Cover Design by Anis Mojgani
Interior Layout by Madison Mae Parker
Edited by Emily J. Mundy
Proofread by Aly Sarafa

Type set in Bergamo.

Printed in the USA

Write Bloody Publishing
Los Angeles, CA

Support Independent Presses
writebloody.com

For my heart.
Which is for me.
Which is for others.
And is for me.

THE TIGERS, THEY LET ME

The Tigers, They Let Me

The Tigers, they let me 17
After Grace Paley 20
Back then 23
Sprig 24
A poem about you and me and the new country 25
With you in this old jalopy of ours 26
Hon or We have both traveled from the other side of some hill, one side of which we may wish we could forget 27
There was a house 28
It was a Tuesday 30
These were my apples 31
When she was young Rilke spoke to her 32
The heart a lump - yellow to gold to gone to green 34
from The fish 35
The 2nd of 2 poems that together and alone speak to a bigger one 41
Addresses 42
Around the hole in his chest 44
Iktsuarpok 45
Hurt I. 47
Cuesta 48
2019 53
Last night 54
I dreamt you twice this week in July 57
It went May, June, June, June, June, October 59
from Simply 62
Three days before I watch her climb the rocks on the other side of the river to stand in line before jumping in 63
Moving her mouth with mine 66
Wobbly 67
The 1st of 2 poems that together and alone speak to a bigger one 68
In this brief expanse of earth are we not all little poems of fruit and love and sex 69
Hemming my shirt in your basement 72
Coming to Cape Lookout for the second time 73
Over the hill my heart 74
The Junes 76
The blueness of the heart in the dream 78
December 30, 2021: the string of the beads 81
You are freckled like spring 86

Things I love 87
Willamette & Clackamas 89
Translation of a song from somewhere else I do not remember 91
Across from where the rhododendrons grow 94
In January 95
2021 96
The deer... 98
In the mouth of 101
Snow & cardamom 111
In Paris, with you..112
Chalcedony 114
Hurt II 115
Somewhere in the bend 116
To the sea 117
Marseille I. August's End 118
In summer 121
Acknowledgments 125

*You are what you love, not what loves you.
That's what I decided a long time ago.*

—Donald Kaufman

The tigers, they let me

the tigers
they let me

touch them

they were so soft

even when
out the front door
they left
with their softness

even when

they left
with my arm

even when
seemingly too
like a puppy
holding but a plush whale
squeaking
in their mouth

it's not that it didn't hurt

but there was no blood
and another arm arrived
from out of my body
like a daffodil
out of the winter
and now—

well
i have one arm

and

at the same time

i have two arms
and
at the same time

i have many arms
all the arms

that have been taken or lost or given

i have them too
still somewhere
under the earth of me

and they

being unseen

being but a memory

are able to touch

what isn't there
but there still the same

able to lift what is invisible

and there are a lot of tigers
in the world

to be touched
from afar

their softness

a lot of tigers
whether flush with rich fur
or belly waxing and backs bowed meeting
in the middle broken-
toothed and belly
concave

as a waning
moon──there are
                lots of tigers

and many
flowers
of petals   jugs
of burnt clay   clouds moving
over pastures and songs
made rich by the throats
loving them into loudness
made rich from the earth
up to the elbows planted
and pulled into
the third month's end
softening

it takes a lot of arms
a lot of arms

to touch us all

i am a tiger too

Little heart. Sweet little heart. You do not need to thrush so, no need to loud song yourself from under the brush. Sweet-winged self sit softly. You don't need to thrash. Someone else will come, who will not take your feathers in their lust for flight. Who will not clip another's wings & call it a letting go. I know that you wish for others to embrace sky, to share that sky. But you can only point at the clouds & show how your heavy feet too are trying to lift. Little heart, you can only offer up water, not thirst. Another will drink, & without taking. Others already do. Little heart. How loved you are, in ways you forget or do not see, eyeless & beautiful, you make your way still through. Oh little heart. That I could lift you out my chest, hold you in my palms' hills, & let you know how safe & already loved you are. Touch the wanting you want so much to give away to others, kiss you, & set you gently back into the body of my own being. Little heart. It is morning. Do you feel it here? There is no need for dreaming. Lead me. Tell me where to follow you, & I will.

Back then

When the wildflowers became from the rain's arrival and departure. When spring was leaving and summer was only beginning. When the Texas sun was not at its terrible apex. When the lake at dusk found their mouths and gave them dark lips. When the canoe wrote the poem with an arrowhead wake. When all movement was a holy dance. When the island gathered lovers like cat's eye marbles in a drain. When the sinks in heaven filled full. When two bicycles became church. When he prayed hard enough for the gods to actually hear his heart. When the thunderstorm kept her plane on the runway. When he pulled the car off into the gravel and grass lot of a barbecue joint off Ben White Blvd. to take her call with the sky's water falling like sheets of metal. When he turned back to the airport to pick her up and bring her back home. When he was new again. When he became fearless. When he walked the middle of the street and no car could touch his joyous bones. When she was nervous out loud laughter, was knots happy for his fingers. When she was the sweetest meat of every plum. When under his touch she became water, was juice on his chin. When all the orchards parted for the song of her heart to sing between their branches. When she knew a tree they could grow together would be planted. When she dreamed of their children's names. When the scorpions stood still in awe of this dreaming. When the gods silently undressed to step into the coldest river. When the heat of their bodies made the steam rise. When their nakedness was a gentle wonder. When the elbow sang. When the ear, the back of the leg, the gentle neck, her mouth. When what their bodies sung too, sang back. When the corners of the country bowed before them. When, like race cars in love, they barreled across every map. When Traverse City, when Chicago, when Puget Sound. When the evergreens broke the rain. When she took him to the graveyard. When he lay on her chest. When he used the grass to whisper his love to her and placed his head on her belly less an offering to an altar and more a release of anything earthly. When all the grief his fists clenched became dust and the wind spoke. When tongueful they understood the words, and anything in him missing stayed missing, and he had no need for its return. When the world became small enough to hold. When her and him were her and him, and her and him was all the magic a magical thing needed. Oh, what a plum it was. The tight skin peeling back from their bodies, and blackbirds pouring out as sure as song.

Sprig

In the dark I followed
your birds. They brought me

here, to this spruce. See
the sprig of it, brought back to you

that I am holding in
my hand? It is from your tree

—oh sprig of my heart

I have broken
off for you.

I saw your heart
when you thought
no one would

you saw my heart
when I thought
no one was looking.

I saw yours

smiling at that color
of turned yellow you love
when your heart thought
no one would

look.
We are all walking home

on the backs of our ancestors.
"In here," he said,

pointing to his chest,
"You smell like spring."

A poem about you and me and the new country

O, the glorious fightings I would start for you

I wish to hold you in this bed forever
the blue wilderness on your tongue
the country of your arms
this is my body worshipping

a new country of light
stamping our passports as we pass

what a sound my spirit makes
when I am not looking
like a zipper opening up an ocean

the Eiffel Tower bending towards the earth to tell it a secret

pushing a flute
out of the bone of your lips is a mystery
what mountain birthed your heart

you are such magnificent poems

I want to rub my face all over you

later when standing in the kitchen
breaking the eggs for you
you call out
and say what a lovely sound

With you in this old jalopy of ours
after Jeremy Radin

And even though the storm comin up behind us sounded like a platoon of harpies scrapin shovels across their iron hearts hard enough to make the strings scream, I didn't even look over my shoulder. We were sittin, all blueberries and yellow light, at the breakfast table when that wind first came up hard fast and howlin over the hill like a whole countryside of ghosts crammed into a padlocked barn. When they started shakin the windows, I kept pourin the maple syrup. When they split open the chimney, I put another spoonful of sugar in my cup. But by the time they started liftin the roof, my teeth were rattlin like the pages of a book in a hurricane. But baby my heart was still as a flag folded under glass. It's cuz my palms, they don't bleed anymore. They're clean. I'm a desert after a hard rain. For a long time I carried bandages from my last knife fight. But with all them poltergeists comin into my house and touchin at my stuff and pokin at my elbows—pleadin for me to bend, achin me to break, beggin to be let back in to haunt me like they used to—I pushed my chair away from the table, peeled the papers off my body, grabbed the magnolia that sure as June follows May is your hand and threw every switchblade under the tractors. We got the old car started and down the hill drove chuggin along with that jalopy cursin loudly, belchin up oil and steam, that gale of wailin sprits tried I tell ya, to give chase. Hell, they did give chase. Poured out the hills like they was mad bees made of hate and thin-tusked bone, soundin like metal on metal, like bone was cuttin through bone, soundin like a city eatin itself through its skyscrapers, angry and hungerin for somethin softer to fill itself with. They swarmed all around the car tryin to get in, stabbin their bodies through the car like it was butter in Georgia. They tried to lift us up into whatever dark world they had poured out from. They failed, darlin. Well, they maybe got those tires a coupla feet off the ground, but nothin more than that—hell, we were just too damn heavy, you and me. Weighed down in whatever it was we two had found inside ourselves and then built between one another. We cracked the spine of our love like a whip. Turned those phantoms into clouds. Clouds of loud screamin power. And had those horses called ours, carry us all the way into town.

Hon
or
We have both traveled from the other side of some hill, one side of which we may wish we could forget

Love me stupid.
Love me terrible.
And when I am no
mountain but rather
a monsoon of imperfect
thunder love me. When
I am blue in my face
from swallowing myself
yet wearing my best heart
even if my best heart
is a century of hunger
an angry mule breathing
hard or perhaps even
hopeful. A small sun.
Little and bright.

There was a house

Spent years
like two foals sleeping.

And then like two foals
sleeping and alone.

You saw my skin as a synonym
for the heart and let me in

past the cinnamon coughing
and into the folds of fennel.

The ringing of silver devils
singing bells in the garden
clung

to you
no matter how hard
you wrung

out our old hearts.

Wringing and ringing

finally sounded
the same thing to you
as singing did

and you hungered for quiet.

You lifted my arm

and stepped
past the dog
quaking in her sleep

unlatched the door of no locks
we had made and

climbed
over a fence
that wasn't even there
to hasten

back into the den
that seethes beside the sea.

Entering into the night
I paste back up the ceiling
under the stars

      and once done
peeling it back
to let their soft bodies
back in
I can taste you

in my beard. Every day
is a crossing of shores.

It Was a Tuesday

I spilled like a pitcher of morning sun
tipping over into what had been night. Had risen
at six and was at the convention center by sunup. Eight a.m.,
said poems into a ballroom on East Chavez and before nine
walked out the building's marble steps into the rest of the day.
Watched Apollo break plates over downtown Austin and pour
into Ladybird. I used to live here. Kissed the river with her
and our bicycles. Off my shirt picked the ladybugs. While here
I dropped off divorce papers at the house where she was staying.
Cristin drove me there. Said, *Homie. If you need to rub your junk*
all over those papers before putting them in the mailbox
—no judgement.

Cristin squealed the tires when we left. Under the whispering sky
too blue to speak of. Ate burgers. In the sunlight blood was wiped
from my chin. Later I night-biked through my old neighborhood.
Passing the amber porch at Annie's, I came upon a Halloween party
overflowing with lights and bodies. Both with their ochre filaments
glowing. Like joyful soil in a repurposed urn. Off the porch we spilled,
now like evening sun. All of us did. Flooded our dusk into the night.
Like witches' grins paraded through the thin streets. Found ourselves
outside the Oakwood Cemetery, almost midnight, and the moon
an unstruck nickel. Broke into the graveyard. Broke back out by
kissing my chest to the bottom of the chain-link fence, squeezed
through the space between its teeth and the ground. Just did
what I had to do to move my body back out the deathyard.
Smelled honey. Counted pretty teeth. Scraped cloth but
no skin. And out of the dark dirt pulled a rain lily.
The Texas and October earth was rich with them.

These were my apples

I know they may seem like dark knotted fists
old plums more like potatoes than fruit
the earth has a funny way of loving us
or maybe it is harder than we think
to learn how to give and be given love
it is something I am still learning

on some days her and I were both turquoise
stones in the sunlight
on some days this was the same day
on other days only one of us shining
or only one of us was turquoise and the other a pale jade
as we tried to place that which of ourselves
is something smooth and polished
into the heart of another and the other
knew not what to do
knew not what was being done
what was being offered
was too blinded by the light

perhaps we and the earth
are the same
all these trees
all this water cascading over rocks
under a slow moon becoming a prayer
of birds unfolding over the orange fields
that look as if they are burning

while the sun briefly spills out of her dress
leaving the blue soft dusk of its fabric in our hands
and all we can do as the sun goes into the darkening is try
and hold her fleeting shoulders with our eyes
and the music that our hearts were made to make

When she was young Rilke spoke to her

My mother
gave me books
of poetry because
she knew I loved poems
and she too had loved poems,
while wanting to not
chase me away perchance
simply by stepping towards me
with something we shared
—why is this?
That we so often run
from something beautiful
another offers up to us
even as it is
the very thing
we are holding in our own hands
or the very reason
that we came into the garden
while others slept
that we might pick
the light from off
the fragile leaves
only to be found
by someone
in the night
doing what we all do
loving something
outside of our body
because it makes the something
inside our body
make a sound
that we wish
to hear more of
and this someone
standing across
from us in the garden bed
is standing here too because

they too love something
that sounds like us
and looks like them

The heart a lump –
yellow to gold to gone to green

the gold goes
in order to become
again

like my mother's eyes, green

even hurricane season is changing

I trust still
I do
truly
but maybe
only my family

the hearts of ten or so friends

what music
       in both gentling ways and ways of fire
does for me

and the gunshot
of the leaves
changing to yellow

FROM THE FISH

The morning comes as it does so often—wrapped in bunches of pale yellow velvet clutched to the sky's still breast and with a tired train of blue fabric trailing behind. And I tell myself: my heart is a harp.

A pitcher of syrup sits at the breakfast table. I am in Johnson, VT, living for the month of April with forty other artists. I learn that it takes thirty to fifty gallons of sap for one gallon of Vermont maple syrup. I pour it into my bowl of oatmeal and add milk and brown sugar. Sweet oatmeal makes me think of my father. The milk poured in, Mother, makes me think of you.

How the small can of evaporated milk sat in the fridge of our childhood until cold mornings, when you would whip the porridge with the wooden spoon and then pour the cream in. On the coldest mornings, Mother, you told us to stay warm under the blankets while you laid our clothes for the day over the heater.

It is a cold morning today, when Jenn, Stacia, Katie, and I drive thirty minutes to the neighboring town of Stowe for second breakfast. On the drive, we pass fields blanketed by both late winter and early spring, a conversation happening between ice and grass, between snow and mud. The earth, like it always has, is in the place of figuring shit out.

We pass a house where in the driveway someone has sculpted a fifty-foot-tall obelisk out of the snow. It rises from the ground like frozen thunder, moving between ice white and foam blue. We stop and take pictures. I share them online with the outside world. The water of that world is far from here. The sea, its storms, and all the creatures lurking under its surface. In Stowe, we eat pancakes with raspberries and drink real coffee. We return from second breakfast just in time for lunch.

As I grab a plate and a chair at a large table with my fellow residents, someone smiles and it looks like the smile of a girl in Oregon who I once loved. She curls a ribbon through my head and the heart in my body becomes a harp played by sunlight.

Over lunch I joke with Sallah, telling her it takes eighty gallons of maple sap for one gallon of Vermont sweatpants. Sallah jokes back: it takes nineteen Vermont green beans to make one apple tree. Sallah has seven girls and one son. She sets fire to clay figures and reminds me of you.

The April that I am nine, you and me go to the same park where twenty-four years later I will be wed. You help me put the worm on the hook in the same way your uncles showed you. You show me how to cast the line and wait not for the first tug but the repeated pull from below. I catch two catfish and bring them home. We put them in the fridge. They swim in the bucket; the belly of one is split open and his entrails circle out as he swims. Dead animals we eat or put back into the earth. Dying animals I do not know what to do with. So I close the refrigerator door and leave them in the cold dark to swim on their own. Eventually they die anyway.

Under the dining hall here, flows a river. One can walk down the stairs to the library underneath and from the windows of this lower level watch the river not much farther below. The river here is largely ice. But every day it breaks bits of its frozen body into pieces, sending tiny icebergs south. It is too obvious a metaphor to hold up to the light. But the beauty of this world and the metaphor is that neither truly exists in the other. It all just is. In winter, the water freezes. In spring, it is kissed by the sun.

I tell myself again: My heart is a harp. Played loud. By the quiet sunlight. I think on the love who once loved me, strongly, and who still, went.

Of being left to empty on my own a house of a marriage, and driving to Goodwill the clothes left behind. Leaving me to sink under reddening waves. There are large fish at the bottom of the dark water. The monsters here, they know my name. I have been here before. Because of this, I am trying to fight for the surface. But I am scared. So I stay at the bottom, unsure whether to rise or stay. Here at the bottom I watch the ice form above me.

Mother, the summer night I return home to Oregon from Texas, my heart felt like something out of a movie—walking down the street to get a slice of pizza and calling you just to tell you I met a girl. And how I ain't never done that before—calling you to tell you this. Have almost always been afraid of what color my heart was, what songs it might sing in the key of another's name, and who might hear that music. For the first time in life, all of me moved without fear. All of me starlight, unafraid. All of me beholding my brightness on a platter, offering itself up into whatever future the universe was laying out for me.

When she and I marry two years later, it is a hundred feet from where Father asked you to marry him.

The summer morning after I am married is the quietest my breast has ever known. I am the leaves in May. It is Sunday, and no one is on the street but me and my new bride. We walk out of our room on Magazine Street, hearts wet with one another, and buy a toothbrush and toothpaste at the corner gas station. We stand over a sewage drain in front of the most expensive restaurant in town and take turns brushing our teeth together for the first time as wife and husband.

The autumn night she decides she isn't ever coming back home, my body is a piano with no strings, attempting to wail but only making splinters. I eat barbecue with my closest friends and cry in their arms. I stare at a wedding present hanging on the wall, take our dog for a walk, and think about driving to the gulf, what my body might taste like in its mouth. The morning that comes is the first of many bright and dangerous ones.

The autumn morning I call you from a hotel room to tell you that I am scared I will kill myself on one of these days, is a fire that stays burning in my head. But I am trying to unlearn the fish in the fridge. To pull out the creatures in me I would rather bury in the dark. To not be afraid of who sees my colors or hears my music, no matter what shade or what note they may be coming from. So I say out loud to you that death is an ocean, and I am not wading into it, but I can see it from where I stand, can taste its salt in the air, and I am scared of how close the sound of it crashes. How quickly fear returns us to the place that birthed it.

You tell me how long ago, before any of us were born, before you had met my father, when you were younger than me, you were in the same place. How lost and forgotten in the world you came to be. Swallowed by the big fish, cut out of the monster's belly, you floated to the top, fought your way back to dry land, stepped out of the water, and sat feeling the sun in the sky, clutching the bunches of your soft and tender self to your feathering breast. How close you came to letting the tired train of life trail its way out of you.

In Vermont, before dinner, for fifteen minutes I paint my heart smooth. I lay beautiful colors next to beautiful colors, similar to how the sky and the sea speak to one another with no measurement of lines, and try to remember a year is not a year. It is only the seasons repeating their passage into one another. Tomorrow will be snow. And then rain. And then sun, unbuttoning the river's winter coat. By this week's end the river will be completely unfrozen. The water will crest off the rocks like a great dance. This is not a metaphor. This is what happens.

After dinner, eleven of us gather downstairs in the lounge with popcorn and watch a movie from our childhoods. Across the heavens above us, I can hear someone in heavy boots walking hard. The water some mornings, is warm and light on my ankles. Some mornings it is red and up to my neck. But sitting in it right now, I know it is nice to be human in the company of other humans while laughing. There are not many nicer things than this.

After the movie, I lie under my sheets with the lights out. The wind blows so strong that the windows rattle like a roof. I feel the whole earth shake like a ship. Such a deep low creaking outside this little but still room. Its stillness is a prayer walking up the stairs. It sounds like the inside of a lighthouse without the sea.

Much like this stillness, I came through you in the late night. Touched my first morning against your chest. All the beasts in the streets brightly burning the clouds with their orange flanks. We are moving beneath their beautiful bellies, not yet swimming inside them. So many creatures of the deep purposing themselves to swallow so many of us. Whole or in pieces, as we so often quietly are taken. I am scared, am more scared of being quiet, so I tell myself that the animals with jaws are also maybe scared. Maybe even, not even monsters, just things with skin that breathe too. So until I can sit with you beside the southern waters, take this, Mother, as I too promise to take it: the sun birthing itself above us like it did then, as it does every morning—clutching bunches of pale yellow velvet to its still breast. Let us watch the furred and legged ones come to the water to drink, as we do. Watch the fish come to the surface to nibble at the day just the same as us. Let us learn when to pull them up. When to pull the hook out. When to let them go.

The 2nd of 2 poems that together and alone speak to a bigger one

I worked hard
under the hot iron
of someone else's
love become terrible
and my own rebuilt
hands   and heart
learning again and
first time   how
to hold softly
my soil of self
in the pull and patience
of seasons   own seeds
thrown   and sewn
under my till   my plough
my swords mine
bent like a note
by my own grit
and doing to sing
these soft petals
of self   and   love
that the inside of me
has at times clutched
too hard to be heard
coaxed by the tongue
of another to speak
from beneath these stones
of this hearth
my heart's earth
by way of their
daylight coming
in under   showing
I   can let it in
and too let out
      my own
   gentling
buds

Addresses

My most beautiful wedding was on a hot day under the magnolias
and after birdseed was thrown into our laughing mouths

sticking itself to the sweat on our limbs, we crossed Magazine St.
and in the warm water of the tub I lowered
my kiss between her knees. *Darling*

is the word she once used to name me *home*.
Some of everything was once hers but not everything ever was.

Everything of mine is mine—

feeding pancakes to the birds off the Bleeker St. fire escape
the way the -30° night in Fairbanks froze my nose hairs

the moose I saw past the glacier   my birthday breakfast
of ice cream and Oreos
the morning after turning thirteen   the snow-colored constellations
                                of the clouds moving over Salvadore
as a nation dressed in white set flowers down
into the waves on New Year's Eve
                            kissing Emily
    against the sink top in a hotel bathroom in Augsburg

Sarah taking baths on Barbur by candlelight   the fox
                                my sister and I saw
off Lake Michigan one Fourth of July
my sister telling me to not get too close as it looked sick
how it and I stared   and I cannot recall
who disappeared first and now   how by way of me
remembering the fox

the fox always comes back

how always the flock in the sky curves
like a sail
        billowing
                to fullness

in the wind of my heart

Around the hole in his chest

There was a hole in his chest
for the birds to fly in and out of
and he had a tattoo of a robin on his neck
and if you put your hand upon it it was warm
and in fractured light one might swear they saw it stretch its wings
and he asked me if I wanted one
and I said yes
and so he took a bird fresh from inside into out
and cupping it
and opening my mouth
I placed it inside
softly so as not to crush or scare it
and slowly swallowed
I can feel it there
on some days
in me
moving
in me

Iktsuarpok

I excite about the rose in my body becoming

•

I do not know what to say to you
in the space between goodbye
and the click of the phone

the clicking of the closing car door
the wet place I must travel
between my chest and my tongue

•

When the one in which Motown seems to lift goes to say
farewell for the day
and the two of you
open your mouths
and do not utter *I love you*
but *I*—

I hope you…?

•

What word do we have in English as the preamble to love?

Might it get more o's or less?
I looooov you?
I lcve you? Half-moon your half-moon I do?

Or is it something else?

Neither high tide or low
but whatever that was empty
becoming unemptied,
becoming filled
a coming into

a gaining of shape
and becoming defined
when your eyes look upon my face—
I
unfurl beautifully you

I flag in the wind slowly you

I shudder but flutter
under the leaving of you

•

There is an Inuit word for the anticipation one feels when waiting
for their love to come over to their house

What does the captain say to the sea when stepping onto the shore?
What does the captain's love say to them
when the captain goes back on the boat?
What color the kerchiefs that flap from the top of their home?

It is something like this

That even with not wishing to say goodbye
I am already excited for your return

What have I been waving while waiting here beside these cliffs?
What is it that I have been saying to my heart all these years?
How it just wanted shape again

as I walked the corners of my roof
watching the ocean like a clock
waiting for my heart's return from afar
pacing the edges
staring at the horizon
mistaking the rising moon for a familiar sail
giving the stars their definition
simply by looking at them
what was in my mouth looking to be known?

What is in yours of which this knowing could be found?

Hurt I.

I love your face

I see it
and it hurts

inside me

much in the way
I imagine

maybe the earth
hurts

in its breaking

when out of the ground
and into the world

spring cracks in

Cuesta

As she held me she wished

in her pocket

she could keep me

I wished

the same

but it was daylight

and I had to catch through that light a stupid plane

and fly northerly when

from her hands so soft the fruit

she had sliced

for us I took

in my mouth already

it an echo

of me needing to leave

already

blooming in the field of

this poem not yet

arrived I

took a picture of her

the night before

sitting in bed smiling

at me happy to be

there with the lamplight's light

before when

through the night

we turned

in towards one another holding

and then away

familiar

like tides and

again the returning

like waves

natural

like the early days

of both our marriages

a valley before

the butting

into the steep side climbing

a hard spine to the sky

and back in

by way of the ridge's gentle side

—after so many years since you and I

were young in another city

somehow still remembering the other

there and here wanting

to keep loving

you—I took

a second photo

in the morning of her hands

a knife with strawberries gentle as a child

her eyes

dark almonds

as if this was

how it always was

how it could be

a blooming

outside the back door

a tree of oranges

in the soft light

her hands

leaking

onto me

as I gently

under them

—as we gently

under each other

moved

sloping softly

to touch earth again

2019

There was snow in February, and it was beautiful. I went down to Texas and watched Sarah and Matty get wed. Loud-smiled beaming she was, and his face round as the word joy. Texas was cold that week. And we, in the wind, played baseball. Back in New Orleans, after three years in my sister's basement, my parents moved back into their own home. It now has a tall staircase that reaches a whole story that didn't exist before. From its windows—windows that were only air before—I can see parts of the oak tree beside the house that I never could before, parts of sky before then unseen by me, nor any of my family. My 13-yr-old nephew and I shared many delicious foods. Coconut shrimp and sweet potato shredded. Carrots seasoned to taste a way I didn't know carrots could be. Then April came west and in a town beside the Oregon coast I heard the elk sing. We drove past a grassy lot on the way back from picking up groceries and there they were—what, twenty of them? Just sitting there beside an old shed against an older sky, still but singing their strange curling whistle that I had never before heard and me and Adam and Matt were confused in the best way, and later Jeremy saw them calmly and effortlessly jump the fence of a baseball field on their way to wherever it is they went after coming from wherever it is they had come from. Me, I found a sand dollar on the beach, unbroken by the ocean's crashing. In summer, I finished writing an opera about Blackness. In fall, I finished writing a picture book about death and how we learn to haunt each other, what it might mean to haunt and to be haunted, how the word haunt comes from *to be back home*. In November, I was given a night of dancing in a stranger's garage with five people at two in the morning, walking home afterwards with two of them, over the city's dormant volcano to get there, sliding down the slope's north side to walk down Belmont St., to be invited inside the room of a pretty woman and fall asleep with her in my arms and reading Neruda in the shower and watching her pour water from a hot kettle into the tub and the vines watching us kiss, and falling into the arms of a tornado spun from two spun hearts, spinning together carried far in the same spot, to be brought somewhere that I had been before and also for the very first time.

Last night

About twenty minutes before the last of the day's blue light emptied out of dusk's overturned bowl, I hopped on my bike, and it felt like I was in Savannah again. Twenty-two years old on empty streets and with no destination but whatever corner I turned at, with this Portland evening twilighting the sky like it was lake water and Venus up there alone in the depth, bright like a needle, Maurice Ravel in my headphones plucking out his piano, looping down NE 28th and across Burnside to bike back through the darkened church parking lot, passing the string lights hanging there in the lit leaves like the high end of the white keys, moving through the now night like a memory and then sitting with Emily and Matt—them sitting on their stoop, me below, held under the many ribbons of the still weeping willow that sits on the sidewalk—and I couldn't touch the two of them nor see their smiles under the masks and the darkness, but this is what it is now, so it was okay and better than alright 'cause I had started my day with iced coffee and a glazed pastry, and Sarah and I then rode our bikes to go see Joy and the kids and the wonder that is the fourteen-foot-tall agave plant that this week was flowering on Glisan St. for the flower's first and last time—bloom the color of a bruise threatening blood to become known—and then before dinner I drew alone in the garage a comic strip about a moon and a man and then stepped out into the bluest hour, and now night was here, with a porchlight on behind us—their door the color of a mandarin—and the wind here too, swooping in to love us in only the way the wind knows how to—loud and touching like a laugh you laugh at—and I tell you even with no one out it felt like Friday, riding loudly down the middle of 28th on my way home, out loud singing a song sounding like sweet milk sung underneath the traffic light at Belmont, before falling asleep on the couch and waking at two a.m. to head upstairs and text Han to tell them, g'night love you before falling into bed with that same loving wind rocking me to sleep—and it was perhaps the sweetest Friday I've had since this goddang world went and changed six weeks ago everything about how it lifts us up and sets us back down.

I DREAMT YOU TWICE THIS WEEK IN JULY

In the first dream the waters came
down from heaven's corners
and you smiled as they flooded
over you smiling and over
your head the water rose
and still you were smiling still
you were okay with all this

In this dream my lover's small white dog
who died a week and some days past
was sitting inside an unlit fireplace
and I carried little Olive across the stones of the room
to her owner   this woman whose skin
has been my summer blanket
whose lips and kindness I am constantly
                like the reddest leaf falling
        struck by

And the water that was covering your brow
in the dream
began to recede and came back down
over your cheeks still round and smiling
while other dogs in the room were also returned
from and to somewhere
and the rain kept leaking out of the sky

Until it leaked out the world of the dreaming
and into my waking one
where the rain was falling
outside the walls of my love's house
and in the morning as my mouth
moved over my lover and my hand
moved inside her my thoughts too
drifted back to you
                with me having just woken
from the second dream
in which you
were so cruel

I could not
once in the waking
pick myself back up

And the woman in whose bed I woke
—in the dream she pulled me away
from the party you were throwing
which seemed to be thrown
only to humiliate me
to make me small
and she
           this lover who in real life
         on the interstate stops the car
   to forage flowers
grabbed me like one
pulling me behind her like the tail of a comet
and out the front door we raced
leaving it swinging behind us
running with our jackets clutched
out into the night us laughing
her hand around mine
hopping into some small car
parked outside to make our escape
tires burning through and over
the earth curving under the pines
bending by way of the stars
constellating above
the panting of our laughter
our jackets still clutched
in one hand and in the other
each other's fingers held tight
like our hands
could shuck the corn silk
from off one another's pasts
and with her hand in mine and mine in hers
we let the steering wheel take the road
to let our other hands hang
a moment out the window
to open our palms
of the jackets they held
and let go

It went May, June, June, June, June, October

her in the tub calling *i'm here*
upon me coming into the house
and through the bathroom door her smile
coming out of the steam the freckles
across her cheeks and shoulders rising
out of the milky bath
like pebbles becoming
an archipelago in the hot air
i kiss her shorelines
her lips i love
so much our smiles
becoming one my face wet
from hers
up to my wrists
my hands in the water
her elbows
our selves deepening in the wet together
while outside the bathroom's wrinkled window
the figs on the tree in the yard
were not yet then in bloom
when they grew on the smaller tree up front
like a bruise becoming a flower
but still in the before of the blossom
purple and heavy with seed
blanketed by sweet
she brought me some
from the bowl she filled with them
they were better than knowing a poem by heart
they were a poem
known by the heart
she picked more
and we sliced them together
into small bits
laid them out on the layers of pans
and she dried them out overnight
they were so soft
so delicious

nothing cold about them
but they were not plums
but a different poem
from a different tree in her yard
this still was in summer
perhaps and probably
after or before
a day we swam
jumping
off the hot stones
like we were somewhere in the mediterranean
and not milwaukee oregon leaping
into the green wide place of the river
where it bends past the big houses
curves around elk rock
and heads south into the sun
where we
would kiss
upon rising from under the water
our faces wet
climb out of the waves made
from the boats passing
to sit and marvel
at the beauteous height
of the stone wall that rises on the other side of the river
like we were swimming
outside a palace
escaping its shadow
for the kingdom of our own sunlight
which let the day
dry our skin warm
and then
jump in again
what a marvelous time
june is
the month of both our births
a month of both our hurt hearts
birthing themselves again
especially when the month stretches itself
through the months to follow
as if again
birthing itself again

side by side
in the splash
rising like freckles
out of the water
waving
becoming
archipelagos
islands
that curve
towards and
under the water
connecting
into one another

FROM SIMPLY

I have loved her like the stars coming out

Ursa's paws pushing down on the dark quilt

as easily as the cat stepping over the cushions

I have loved her

like how the buds in May
can do nothing but awaken
under the fingers of spring

I have loved her

like how the figs swell
and how the plums fall when full
and how rubbing rosemary leaves its scent

upon our thumbs I love you—as easy as this
as easily as *her*

just now and here became *you*

Three days before I watch her climb the rocks on the other side of a river to stand in line before jumping in

On the hottest day we went to the ocean.

On the drive we listened to songs and some we sung along with.

We told each other about our mothers.

Between our seats we held together our hands.

I had never been to Cape Lookout before.

We climbed over rocks to get closer to the water.

We got closer to the water to go in.

I brought the top of my head under.

Let the Pacific wash its salt over me.

I watched you go farther and farther into the loud waves.

I made sure Mae didn't go out too far to try and get you.

I made sure tiny Olive didn't get swept out to sea by the tide.

You returned.

And under the high rock we laid down our towels on the sand.

We pulled out the books we had bought that morning.

The sun showed up warming our limbs.

The clouds moved quickly over the sky.

I watched them, and the drops of water on both our skins.

The corners of our pages in the wind flicked like quick wings.

Our feet kissed one another.

Like how a breeze pushes the flowers together.

When we had had enough, we pulled back on our shirts.

We climbed back out over the rocks.

Sat at a picnic table in the dunes while Mae sniffed the tall grass.

Olive shivered in your lap as you warmed her under the towel.

I read out loud to you Derek Walcott, his poem "White Egrets."

I think perhaps this was when I first started

to quietly let myself fall in love with you.

We took the wind with us when we left, a cooling for our skin.

It held without stretching the heat of our hearts.

Into the reddening sky we drove.

Headed into town to fill our bellies under the sinking sun.

We sat in a half field waiting on burgers out of a cart to be done.

I took a picture of you I love.

You in a shirt you had dyed the color of an ocean in a painting.

Your smiling lips being dyed in the orange light.

How warm the setting sky was on us as we ate.

Like it needed to leak out the last of its heat before going.

We began again like people always do.

Like threads sticking up. We offered each other to pull.

To unravel what our befores had been. To see underneath

what was. What had once been woven over.

A reconfiguring for our constellations.

We spun closer.

I keep returning.

To the spool of light.

Its starkness against the dark, still

somehow soft.

Moving her mouth with mine

How the rain came out of nowhere
and while getting water from the sink
looking out the window in the kitchen
at the yard that had been so yellowed,
so thin and thirsty so recently, now seeing
the wet grass darkening under
this late summer rain, with surprise
I said to you Look how dark the rain
is making the yard, how green, so green
and you smiled with agreement
my love—where did all of it come from
—all that water, all that color,
all that grass was just waiting there
for the water to fall, the grass
thirsting, waiting for the water
to come and all this water
just waiting from somewhere
came to give a drinking
came to be drunk
and was drunk

Wobbly

It is nice to take the late afternoon
to tape down the trim and the edge of the doorways
in the room she is painting upstairs in her home
and to stop before we are finished before she leaves
to get a drink with her friend and to touch
our mouths instead wet against each other
to touch her lips with my fingers her thighs
with my hands moving under the clean dress
she has just put on lifting skin clenched
her leg and her hands running beneath
the button of my waistband her thumb
unbuttoning and me unzipping so she
can lift me out to press myself
into her and have the two of us fuck
in the doorless closet
of the second floor's doorless room
while the neighbor's chatter lifts through
the windows open and her roommate's
phone conversation just around
the corner's thin wall and down
the hall coming
in the direction of
our silence fighting against
our own breaths hard as our limbs hard
pressed to the walls primed
freshly and outside is still the day's shine
like a shoulder thrown from under a coat
with us here both trying
to cum quickly and us
smiling like knife light
loud on the inside my palms
tight around her hips
she opening her body
her body a shiver gives and a
tremor both and a shaking both
run through her
and over me

The 1st of 2 poems that together and alone speak to a bigger one

Yesterday afternoon half asleep
in my bed whispering
into your ear I said
I like it when you
come into a room I am in

In this brief expanse of earth are we not all little poems of fruit and love and sex

come your hands my love how purple they are

dripping from your own touch purple love my teeth

like a plum from the tree pluck the breath of your chest

the plum will not grow more sweet once pulled

at the place it was when pulled

what sugars right now are in your breasts

what sugar in me is under your tongue

is my sugar the plum in your chest

the fig under your skin beneath

your leaves inside our thighs

churning the stingers of my wasps turning them into sugar

a field of cane the stalks split

open silked strands spread and chewed

into wet strings sugared and strung from lip to chin

the red hum in your mouth sugared and sticky running

down these legs where does your neck begin

beneath the biting's end

what of my touch will you suck forth

like a horse on the apple's rind

what of your heart is long swallowed with the soaked

song of your skin in my mouth

what soft fuzz like a forget-me-not curling

under the touch of my finger the moon

circle of biggest longing she watches our hunger

turning our fruit under our teeth

touching in the dark herself inside her own darkness unseen

white light of hers from above falling

cube of sugar in the sky

you dissolving

under the moon your rain

drips down like a river

down me like a river

open yourself like a jug

lip widening open moon

open my mouth like a cup

join in the pouring

june rain coming

under the dew

holding to be wrung

licked soaked

the tongue

stand under the falling

prayers of our own names arrive to us

like the plumped harvest of our bodies

in our mouths hard soft and wet

Hemming my shirt in your basement

In the storms
that whorled unspoken
under your cheekbones
as you sought to stitch
a new floor a roof
that might not lift
in the wind or even
simply a small blanket
of smaller squares
I sought not to quiet
clouds I had no power over
nor to stitch the threads
you needed to on your own
but simply
to be for
        your
at times
shaking
hands
a needle
with the largest eye

Coming to Cape Lookout for the Second Time

Among the trees swinging
in the wind coming in
from off the Pacific
the same trees
under which in June
I read aloud to you
a poem about oblivion
its beauty which
thickens like mist
now in October we are
under their branches
again though now night
and around us the world
so dark I take your lips
in my mouth and your hands
move under my shirt
and over my pants waist
as I pull yours to your knees
and then down
I fall my kiss
to your legs and
between the trees
thickening
my tongue moves
and then down
to the ground
we both go and
into the black earth

Over the hill my heart

and over the hill my heart
goes like shoes in Holland

turned upwards
and

beautifully carved from out of the wood

your face was a stripping of the prayer back to sapling

a transmission of laurel

my heart
cluster of sprigs

your want
a faded twine
that still tied strong

looping gently over my crossed stems

your touch the sun at the river
the sun like a hammer on a plate

and the sun on Mt Tabor when you were
                    in the peach-and-white striped pants
like a slow loving leak towards a gentle oblivion
is how that sun fell

—on the drive from the sunset to your house
you sent a song
from your car to mine
about fucking up sheets

            —moist soil cupped
in a palm to pot
a little plant
joyful soil
once more

overturned and lifting
undressing
the outside undressing the inside of my body

undressing you when you were undressing me
as the day undressed us both

the dusk
my own prayer

soft bag of body clutched

over many meadows to go
one blade at a time

we were bandits of each other—

coming in at sundown while the camp slept
and leading each other away

from the lunchtime embers
still smoldering from whatever
others had turned in the heat

and instead we held

to head to the tall grass
and weave

    for a short sit
    at the loom of what we had

    your hand
        in mine my hand in yours
a gentle blanket

The Junes

Even now
with the sadness of the fall
having hurled itself
into the pain of this winter

I still hold what the summer was
and how beautiful a gift
it is to have had
our hearts
mine and yours
to have been naked
in the rooms of ourselves
with one another and touching.
As if June had stretched past her borders
and continued all summer long.
Being with you was like being with flowers.

Being with you was like being flowers

with you and the sun
laying upon my skyward-reaching self.
How close you were on me
it was like no difference
between that which was warm and that which was light,
no lines between what was limb
and what lay inside

and so if I now must have this strange hole in me for right now
of which I know at some point will give way
to something green growing out of or over its depths
even as the depths beneath it might always remain—
if I have to have this now
I will take it
with no thought of exchange
in order to have had
this summer of Junes
   with you.

The only thing I would trade this for
is more.

The Blueness of the Heart in the Dream

The boom happened earlier.
A gun somewhere in the woods. It is hunting season.
There are elk around here that I have not yet seen,
neither at dawn nor dusk, for I have not been
out on the wet grass at that time though it is neither dusk
nor dawn right now but gentle enough in the morning
to have three deer appear from under the branches of
the hemlock spruce. I see them from my window
and rush gently to the outside to take a picture
and to watch them breathe the same air as I do.
I am holding my heart from afar and yours too
and from up terribly close, trying to be tender
with these quiet wilds and pawing silences.
Why after all these years and times of spying
a deer in the wild or whatever it may be—
something that is part of the earth, as I am,
—moving through the world, that our hearts
might still and always flutter at the excitement
of seeing them in the movement? The geese above
honking over the almost nothing-tailed chipmunk
scurrying, the porpoise breaking the river's surface,
none of this unknown to me and all still bring a smile
to my chest. Like the other day in the marsh,
seeing ever so briefly before it was gone,
a blue heron alighting from the wet brush.

●

December 30, 2021: the string of the beads

1.

Thursday night me and Jenn drive to Burgerville to get fries and burgers. My first excursion to the fast food place in almost four years due to the long strike from its workers. Nothing special but something that allows ourselves to be, and so it was nice to have a little something like that. It feels like an echo of the world we all once lived in, where we would jump into the car like it was still high school and hit the drive-thru for shakes and to bring fries back for people, to return to us moments in our past that held meaning for their being not their doing.

Is life not but a string strung of the moments we live, the thread between the beads of living, that bring us to the next thing of color and weight? It feels that during the pandemic, with so much the same, not only have we been losing the experiences of living, but also that we have lost the moments that fill the spaces between, which in between the living we do, is what our lives are strung of. It is raining, and as we wait in the drive-thru line we search for a Ted Leo song. We bring fries back for others.

2.

Sitting in the kitchen of the Rocketts' home as they ate Chinese food at the table, we unwrapped our burgers and Lilith keeps bringing me bits of Chinese to try. There is a piano in their living room. I ask Jenn who plays the piano and she says Opal, the Rocketts' daughter. Jenn, who lives downstairs in the basement, says her bed is right under the piano so she can hear Opal playing and practicing and for her, she says, it's such a beautiful gift to hear the pieces progress from when Opal first learns them through to when they become her own. Jenn says this is how she wants to view time: as a gentle passage she travels with as it changes and evolves, like getting to hear in it all the parts of it at the same time—the past, the future, the now. Being able to hear it progress in its own beauty towards its own greater beauty.

I want to cry. I think, how beautiful it would be to be able to hold time in such a manner, both the individual notes and the whole piece, the process, path, and fruition all at the same time. How hard it is to lumber and clunk through at times, feeling stuck on the strings between the beads that are sometimes so dazzling while other beads such a weight, pulling your brow down so low that where the beads sit are moments hung in such dark shadows.

I want time to be the beads and also the whole necklace. I want time to be a beautiful piece of music heard from under the floorboards, carrying me from what it was to what it is via what it could be.

3.

Opal comes over to us and listens. And shyly says if we keep talking and don't pay attention to her she will play, and we grin in agreement. She sits at the piano and we keep talking and she plays, beautifully.

I ask Lilith, who is a ceramicist, what pieces in the house are hers versus someone else's. Jenn begins plucking pieces off the shelf that are the work of others.

4.

There are four cups, the work of a Japanese artist, no bigger than large plums. They are white and they glow, shaped as if someone had dried out magnolia blossoms before their time and twisted the petals, as if tissue paper, into small chalices to sip from, the crevices shadowing into tiny lines of cornflower blue, as if plucked from the light of a full moon. The cups' edges are so thin, that when I pick one up, it feels as if I were picking up music. My heart bends inside me so unexpectedly, shocked at how beautiful they were, how beautiful their lightness is. They make me feel just as light. Like how a thin branch might be reminded of its lightness by the leaves it holds and not of the tree whose weight it is also a part of.

I hold the cup in my hands. And being here with my bruised breaking heart, being surrounded by people and tenderness after so long in the pandemic without, and then to have the music Opal is playing, and then having this fragile thing placed in my hands that perhaps is so close to what I feel like inside myself—I feel that if I were alone, would break open from holding the cup. Might have emptied myself onto the floor through water.

The cup is so lovely and beautiful and tiny and tender, as if I am holding a baby, a bird, the heart of either, my own heart from when mine was this size. As if I am this so-small heart I am holding is a heart made out of a small flower or a flower made out of a small heart. It is such a small heart, perhaps the size mine feels right now these days, in the wake of an unexpected turn and leaving. A heart, little and trying to hold on to the big love it feels and holds inside itself, but doesn't seem able to, because that same love is too heavy for this small heart to hold, and so, smaller and smaller it gets, until my own heart were it held in my hands could, like this cup, fit safely between three fingers. And with all this turning inside of me by way of this cup turning in my hands, my heart caves in a little at its edges.

5.

Lilith says the cups are the work of her favorite artist, Takeshi Yasuda, who she was fortunate enough to meet on a trip to Japan years ago.

Eliot brings me some sparkling water to pour into the cup, and I feel like I am sipping from the heart of a ghost. That when we pass from here, perhaps the hearts in us become flowers in our chests, with the color of our lives drained from them but the glow they held when alive still remaining in the skin, and that this ghost heart flower is now in my hands to drink bubbles of water from, that I might not spill all of my own water out of me.

And maybe it is not just that my heart is trying to hold on to the big love it holds, but maybe is also trying to continue being held by the big love that has been holding it; for a branch unheld by the tree is no longer tree. A moment without what surrounds it is just a leaf. Falling.

6.

Jenn is talking about winter, one of her reasons for moving from Maine to Oregon. She is saying that she realized that maybe it's not winter that she hates but rather the discomfort that winter brings, or specific winters, and that it was kind of a big deal for her to realize this distinction.

I sip from the moon flower ghost heart cup, and my heart keeps caving in a little as if I'm walking around with a knife stuck in me—the thinnest of knives, a knife so thin the light doesn't catch it, and I don't feel any pain from it. Just the ever-slight weight of its presence as it sticks out of me, and every now and then some movement of moment in me or some slight breath of moment in the air makes the knife stick a little, and my chest pains and my body winces.

Bill, Eliot's father, says that it sounds like Jenn had an epiphany, and Jenn says yes, it was, it was an epiphany. And Bill says that he's always been jealous of people who have epiphanies, that he would love to have one. And my heart caves in more still—wondering how many folks in the world move through here, either never receiving some sort of clarity dropped into their soul, or never realizing that they already have.

And some sound lifting from Opal's hands or something said from someone that echoes of something else will pull me into a memory of M and the music that was played through me and them this summer, and the knife sticks a little more, and my heart caves in a little further. The moments aren't heavy, but they are still what carries our weight.

7.

I sit there sipping from the ghost flower heart that a gentle man across the ocean pulled out of a fire, and the heart in my chest keeps turning over what Jenn said about wanting all time to progress like the way it does when listening from below to Opal play piano above, and I want so badly for time to be a beautiful piece of music heard from under the floorboards, carrying me from what it was to what it is via what it could be.

Which is what it does—carries us from the past through the future so we can arrive at what is in front of us. Which is what is breaking me these days. I want to be inside the music by being outside of it. I want to be under it, and at the same time, be the song itself but not the instrument that time's song is singing through.

How to give over to the moments between? To let them do what they do, which is be? Like how a note cannot connect to the next, but by way of the quiet that both separates and connects them, allowing the note and the note that follows and the quiet between the two, to all be their own element and all part of the same whole.

8.

I don't have the next bead, the next note. Don't know how long this string is, much less what it connects. Sometimes my strings go off in different directions. So I always worry on how much I take from others, and so have tried for the grown half of my life to make space for those around me. Still, I worry about it all the time, even more so now: whether I am taking from someone else what is a moment of theirs, or, in believing I am sharing a moment with others, am I mistaking what we are sharing, and is it actually only something happening for myself? That we are not connecting at all? That the quiet space I see as the space bridging two notes is just space, with no music made by the quiet between us?

But oh, how in this now world we've been in—one in which there is so much distance between the parts—and this night I now find myself in—a moment with other—is the whole piece of music. And so I sit, with a cup I keep filling to empty into my already fullness, threatening to overflow, believing in the power of shared moments. So many loose threads. No loose notes. Just music being heard through all its arrivals.

You are freckled like spring

It hurt
to have broken this sprig
from off my heart
and give it to you
and to see you like summer
into fall and fall
into winter, go.
It hurts.

THINGS I LOVE

The blues a night sky makes. The bowls it holds for the stars to shine inside of. The sound of a fire moving its tongue against the wood. Riding bicycles with friends. Learning of the lives of others. Getting to know our best & worst birthdays. I love a holy sunset which feels like the sky is praying to me, to us, asking us to look at it & know the fierce colors that lay in its clouds. That even the sky needs but the right hour, the right persons looking up at it, knowing what beauty the sky holds inside itself,
just waiting to pour forth.

I love the crows en masse. Their crossing inside that prayer. Bunched together in their loudness at day's end. Their flight looking like the sky breaking apart to spread itself farther. I love a spreading further in order to come closer. To see what we might arrive at. A wandering with intent. I love not making plans. & making plans. Scheming schemes. Building the idea of an art, like it was a boat becoming bigger upon being greeted by the water it asks to touch its hull. How the ocean wants to hold us but doesn't always know how. I love that even the ocean doesn't know things, even the ocean struggles to move against its nature, & in this way maybe becomes more.

I love colors. How they lay on us & hold us. When they make an object but a plane of their shade. The way they solid & smooth & spill & wash pale or so deep. I love colors so much. How do I love a thing so much that has no form, nothing to touch, simply is? Though I suppose, is this not what all love is? Even an object holding our love is but a placeholder for us to try & with our palms touch the intangible. How the body too is like this. How the love for what it holds infuses what holds the love. How, when the hearts are together in the same space, the bodies become but passageways to the shared place which has no walls to keep the width of our breaths out.

I love writing love poems. More so the living of them.
I love writing in ink a scrap of a note, even as my desk becomes flooded by scraps of notes, whether they say "fuzzy rhythmic vocals" or "a sunflower taught me a poem" or "the emptiness, a missing" or are just measurements of my sleeves.

When the sun lands on one spot, I love this. Eating fruit off a bush on a street or pulled from a tree or fallen from a branch like an offering. Hugging friends goodbye even though I hate goodbyes. When full houses become empty but for me. When an emptied house becomes full again. Learning something new. The thought of sewing a quilt with a friend & their mother. Taking February to begin piano lessons. The piano. I love the piano.

I love when someone plays the piano when you didn't know they could play the piano. When they don't feel they know how to play the piano but there they are in the soft quiet that kisses the two of you playing it, & my heart in this soft quiet is going from bud to bloom to petals on the floor in one breath. I love that people want to share things with each other even when sometimes we do not know how to do this. Is this not too what love itself is—you sharing you & me sharing me & us sharing & being shared with each other? Back & forth?
For whatever length always may be?

Willamette & Clackamas

Strongly and softly, how I loved you

and some days this
is fine—that what was
is what it was

and some days it is not

and in all the days
I am trying

to hold it all like light on linen
and linen in my hands

as a soft thing
held a little less soft by the limits of myself

and so
am trying

to only see
what a niceness it was
                         is

—a kindness
of the world
given to my heart to have gotten
to see you pick blossoms
and dry out marigolds
to string them in a trailer on the coast
to put them in a tin to give to me
holding a bucket in the rain
with you on the roof picking the apples
seeing you awaken in the morning out of your sleep
and you when seeing me smiling
—you saw me—
and reaching your heart towards mine
by way of your kiss
the flowers you gave
to me on my birthday

with only then knowing me
but a few weeks
falling asleep on the couch
wrapped in each other's soft touch
over the summer months
jumping into the rivers
at the drop of a hat together
and how lovingly
for a little period of time
our love fit
the way our bodies did
like those rivers in their banks

Translation of a song from somewhere else I do not remember

At dawn I returned
to your gate

And go through the window
and brighten your face

Say to me my love
something amazing
at the break of day
I will illuminate your face
I will go back to your capture

What you want to tell me
I don't know until you tell me
what you won't tell me I won't know

Come close to my kiss
my love return me
to our capturing
and with my mouth
close your sadness

Our mouths together
lasted for several hours
I got up again with you
in my arms

I go to the window

What a good thing dawn is
it says to us: I will make your face shine
I will return your face to your hands

To the window I go
I will make your face shine

To the window I go
and inside my heart
say good things about you
during all the rest of the day

My love

I have come
to steal you
from the things
that have stolen you
from yourself

I came back to steal
your pain to fling it
under a cloud somewhere

let it fall
like the water of the sea
back into the lake
and pour over the sides
to flood the earth

into new orchards
that grow themselves
to fill us
with what they have

in warm weather grown
to give each other
fruits fat with sugar
flowers full with fragrance
branches for babies to climb

Oh my love

I would have shined your face
from the window
to the floor
and across the room
making every wall
bright enough to be gone

But life has come to steal us

I woke up in your arms again
returned from my abduction of dreams

What a good thing
morning is

I do not understand its meaning
I do not understand the strange words
from my sleeping

I go back to your hands
you will brighten my face

Across from Where the Rhododendrons Grow

I wish I could remember enough of it to make a poem from it: when we walked around Reed's campus with Mae at sunset. I remember it was after dinner, sushi, on Woodstock. I think you had never walked around at Reed before, which surprised me and made me happy, to share in that with you. Though just down the road from where we ate, we drove and parked. I imagine or believe this is what happened, like I said, I wish I could remember enough of it. How green everything was, whatever was around us when I kissed you as I'm sure I did somewhere under the leaves and light. Or you kissed me, coming out of the canyon, on the farther side of the hanging bridge to the area where years ago I saw a coyote cut through the night into the parking lot and where I searched through that field for something a friend had fall from their pocket years past. To the other side we crossed, to where the sky looked like a color you might have made to dye a fabric on your stove or in the garage, pot swirling from hot water into soft pink, like the palms of a white woman soft and old. The sky looked like peach skin, like the softest of knitted threads unraveling from their softness, coloring the field's sparse trees the same sandy shade as your shoulders in summer, and yes, yes I am certain that under the branches of one of them I touched your mouth, because I know I embraced you, and if I embraced you, I certainly touched your mouth, with my lips—for why wouldn't I? How could I not? There, then, under that sky, inside this hour of sunset, as we talked on the sounds of birds, and of chocolates and what we'd eaten, which really is another way of saying that we talked about our hearts for this is what it means to fall in love: to talk together about things that are both nothing and everything, like chocolates and birds and sunsets and trees that cover canyons like hands and walking through handheld canyons as dark comes to greet one's ankles and eyes, and makes the memories of these things a little more hazy, but maybe not so hazy that I, upon sitting down at the edge of my skull's water under the bell of remembrance toning gently above the surface, can't pull enough out of the water, and maybe can pull out enough to make a poem, even if just a little one—a little poem, maybe this poem, or maybe hold just enough of it to have made it enough, for me, us.

In January

The past two days, the sun has made everything the color of a peach. So yesterday Steph, Jenn, and Thom scooped me and we went to Cannon Beach to go jump in the Pacific. We stripped down with our outer layers folded and set on top our shoes and, with Thom watching guard over the tide, we barreled into the surf. And today too, friends were going to the ocean. So I joined to again maybe get in the water but mostly just to go. To be in motion. To be in company. To be able to talk with others or quiet with others. To see the sea. To chase it and be chased by it. To see perhaps anemones. To escape an alone. To escape the shape of self. To fill that which empties. To climb a rock. To touch a rock. To throw a rock and hear it splash in the embrace of it returning to the ocean. To marvel at the sun marveling at me. To seabird. To forget and to remember. To celebrate Lilith arriving at the age of her yesterday. To wonder at the size of the bird that Jenn pointed out to us. To answer Opal of what books I am reading and to ask her the same. To be shared in with all this. To decide to strip down and move the long walk across cold sand to cold water. To freeze my feet in the tide greeting me. To freeze my body in a plunge. To have my feet not warm up in the leaving but to have the sky warm my limbs. The inside of them fueled by my heart that has been racing to outrace itself, running towards some fantasy of a finish line that might arrive from solving its own turning over in my hands, like the waves. But with no crash, only a turning over and over, looking for peace in the hope for a break to come, instead of seeking to just be. To being, in the break of the water as it crashed down into my crouching to grab, lift, and carry me to the shallows. To stand up on cold ankles and a cold chest and a warm pumping of blood between them both. To loud my heart. To quiet my tongue. To revel in people I want to be around, to be wanted by the people around me. To remember. To watch the many bikes going over the sand with the orange rocks climbing upwards on one side of us, and on our other, the sun, slowly going towards a kiss to and from the water. To wish aloud for a man to come up over the sands and sell us hot samosas. To then get in the car and leave Aurora Beach and wind back up the mountain and between the trees and back out and down to watch out the window the country give way to the city once more and call ahead to put in an order and to pick up Indian food and to go inside and sit down and find ourselves eating together the samosas that we had talked about eating together, hot and crunching in our mouths. To go. To go and to go. And to go to be brought home.

2021

Out of one winter and into the next one we went. People in another city gave me a lot of money because they believed in the cogs of my heart. I slept in an A-frame alone in the mountain's woods. Wrote beside its big windows. Cooked breakfast silently. Walked between the broken burnt trees of the state I live in. Fell asleep to the wood in the stove crackling in the cold. Snow fell inside every morning's still, dark coat. Covered everything in feet of itself. And melted by lunchtime. Spring came.

I watched the birds on the ledge hop snow-covered railing to snow-covered railing. Before the blizzard arrived, returned home after weeks away. Came home with mud on my tires. Hung a large poem in large windows. Sat on a rooftop with Cuban shrimp and a woman with eyes like ice melting. In her car, made out for the first time since 2019. Full, we hungered so.

I went to Gearhart to sleep in a house at the coast with my friends, as we have done for so many years before the world changed. Heard Adam laugh and for the first time in 14 months saw his face as it happened. Squeezed Chris' shoulders. Hugged Matt. Walked behind the houses to coffee and pastries. Ate both while going through the dunes to the water. We walked through the tall grass on paths made by the elk. The tide came in and the wind blew hard and the sun shone and the rain came and went again like confetti. Texted in bed with someone back home whose lips wanted mine on theirs. Thought of the icebergs surrounding her pupils and melted a little more. Found a sand dollar unbroken. Returned home on my birthday and touched her face.

Fell naked up the stairs. Went swimming in Mozier to celebrate her birth. Was brought to Cape Lookout for the first time on the hottest day. Touched. Read aloud to someone else. Learned about their parents. Their voice began to memorize itself across my chest. Fell in love, the first time in years. Fell in love in a manner I never have before, with gentle slowness and a giving, like being willed a plot of earth to garden. Had a summer of swimming. Rode many bikes under the sky's dome. The opera I wrote was performed. Listened in the sun to songs that hold both of our hearts. Wrote a dance and danced it alone on a stage in the park near her house on a wet morning. She watched, smiling. I drove to Astoria with a person I loved. We saw Doug Martsch shooting basketball.

From our trailer watched him sing songs that I loved when I was young. Songs Jeff loved too. Songs I still do. She hung a string of marigolds and plucked rose hips from out the dunes.

We camped and cabined. Jumped wild into small waterfalls, lovingly fucked in the tent in the daytime. Returned to Cape Lookout. Fucked lovingly under the trees under the stars on top of the earth. Woke to rain. Our hearts. Hemmed a shirt for the first time under her hands.

Was heartbroken. Saw my family and New Orleans for the first time in two years. Slept alone in the woods by the coast. Bought a guitar before I went. Crossed the estuary in a canoe. Stood with other artists five hundred feet above the ocean. The mist loved us like a map. Held all my broken pieces tight as I could against the cold. The cold still got in. Woke up freezing for too many mornings. Painted in the stillness of me waiting for my tears to fall. Saw three deer run for the moss. Walked through the dark afraid of mountain lions. Came back home. Winter arrived. Struggled like a rock, to stay with the whitecaps. Winter stayed.
And spring came. Again.

THE DEER

My heart is a deer
walking across a lake
in winter. It is cold
but this means
he can make it across.

If it were spring
the hooves of my heart
through the ice would fall.

My heart is a deer
leaving no trace on the lake
he has just crossed—
what he walked over
is now only river. Snow
from the mountains

now water, filled with fish
going from where they were born
in the direction of home.

In the mouth of

I have traveled far

I climbed over the animals

and sometimes laid still

that they would climb over me

did you do this too?

did you get stuck in the jaw

the maw

of the moon cawing

in the sky bright white silence

crawling through?

•

I wanted to have someone to love who loved me too

•

the things we seek for our loved ones to learn,
are often the things we wish to teach ourselves

•

color of the bloom

even when bloomed

bloamed

always I am in love
with the gloaming

•

I am under the blades of the field machine

I am in the warm water up

to my chin cold rain falling

I cup

my heart like a lotus flower

carrying petals in a palm of water from kitchens to rivers

I clench my heart like a thought and falter

I clench my heart like a stone to hurl at all tanks

am clenching it like a shawl inside a fall turned frozen

clenching it like fists at a funeral

pallbearer

what weights still holding inside the box?

•

this world was always gonna break your big heart

•

how wide the lake
of your heart?

how far the shores of it?

how tired are your arms from rowing?
how strong? how do they keep going?

•

love is bearing witness to someone's learning and unlearning of self

even if in the unlearning is the unraveling of any threads of their shawl that bear your colors

•

I remember nightfall

when it came

caught by the black spark

in the back of the dark

my heart was a summer night

wet and hot and cooling off

the toads an opera

lifting between the oak's arms

with the charmed perfume of the magnolia

I remember nightfall

when it came like a minotaur

and my heart the ball of string used to find my way
back out of the maze of dark corners

and was the string pulled back with me

in following the wake back to the break

or was it left behind in our escape

I told someone I love yesterday

do that which is the best blurred and balanced line

between what will bring you the most joy
and will be the least complicated

I want my actions—my choice—like a tree

the least complicated / most joy

does the moon howl in a note too high to be heard
or low enough to be the most silent?

what is the difference between being unheard and keeping quiet?

there is a difference and both differences have to do with another

•

I traveled while carrying far

my heart so tight they would have had to break

two of my sharpest teeth to pull it out

of my mouth

I carry my heart in my mouth

like the wolf's it is the safest embrace

and I am bringing it through this world to somewhere

where it can be

and I want it to arrive whole

is what I told myself without telling myself

•

*Anis
is love not but a bearing witness
to another's unlearning of what they are
& giving them the space, unafraid, to do so?*

*Anis
is love not but allowing another
to bear witness to our own
unlearning of self, & in the face of the fear
that they may go as a result of this?*

•

I had a dream and then I died

and I died in the dream
and was still there

in the dream

and I woke up

•

I had a dream and then I died

underneath the vulture's belly

I was a scared golden that the lightning bolt kept

searching for feathers it was in feathers I was

no longer wet only storm

in me was the storm outside looking

the ways in which the windows would bend

in the wind creaking my heart creaking
like the floor under my weight

small as I was small as we all were

•

in the passing of light and the passing of night
when the dark gives shapes and no lines
is the wolf only a hound?
is the hound actually a wolf?
what jaws will carry me?

•

Listen Anis:

burn any flag that doesn't blow by way the wind of your heart
burn any flag that don't blow by way of your heart's breath
burn any flag that doesn't flap from your own gale

•

answer the question your self is asking you

all that I make is an effort to find the question

for the languageless answer my self is

•

What answer is the least complicated?

•

how large was my heart to carry all my days inside of it?
how many days did I have in my mouth?
how many days have I swallowed?
how many days do I still have to eat?
how do the flowers measure their hour
bodies bending themselves naked towards the light
and closed at night like a church door in the dark?
there is stained glass in the arch of my heart
there is a stone in my body that my body
is making a breaking of color to make music from
there is a song in the cracking of windows
in the smash
in the crash
the waves like my mother
utter my name even when I am not beside them

•

The least complicated / and the most joy

•

call the blanket a dance

call the sky a blanket

call the wrapping of it around me a dirge

call your touch the same

pocket of blossoms

pocketful

at times tenderness still becomes forgotten

what of us is already becoming history?

there is a door on my arm not yet constructed

perched upon the moon's steeple

I am two-stepping to a cloud to come home

what cloud is bridging between my years

that has never moved?

there are bombs that fall

in actual cities where actual children wake in the falling

right now

they fall

what of us is already becoming history?

my language is being woven even as it comes undone

who will bear witness to my unraveling?

who will stay when it comes?

I wrote in my head the other day

: *you are an avalanche before the song*

we are witnessing the end of snow

what avalanches are coming that we cannot see?

the earth unlearning itself of us

fuck your dry mountains

as I said before: *at times my tenderness becomes forgotten*

sometimes it is remembered and then flung

still, a pocket full of blossoms

is love not but a bearing witness to another's unplanting?

is love not but allowing another to bear witness

to our own new system of roots

and in the face of the fear that they may go because of such?

I keep trying to turn my tongue into my mouth

but it just turns in my mouth

underneath my heart

moving like a salmon in these rivers

back and forth between the mouth and the source

Snow & cardamom

What a powerful tree it was.
So green its young and becoming leaves were.
And still turning greener. There were birds flying towards it.
I will work to leave the tree where it was. Even if we are not there,
the birds will one day arrive. It is okay if there were times we believed
we did not plant it. I know your hands were there in the dirt with mine.
It will one day be okay that we had to leave to wash our palms.
It will one day be okay if we had to trade our arms for the soap.
I know that we loved the warm smell of the earth. I know the bodies
we are given, in some parts of our lives are harder to carry
than in other parts. It will be okay if we alone do not ever again
travel through that land where in the gray and singing wind
this tree sways softly. I know it sways. I know the rain falls there.
I know the sun touches the dark clouds and the seasons pass through,
each one visiting with the tree's quiet body for a short spell
of cardamom and snow. It will be okay if never do we see
what fruit still grows from its heart. I know
our trees will be here a long time.
Longer than we or I or any of us will be.
Like the light falling out the stars, soil
shifting through our bones
the eternal machine of night
and day keeps turning—
the cherry pits split
cracking open orchards
into a quietless world.
And amongst the noise
of their fruit falling like a gift
their shape taken
over time giving shade
from the sun to any of us
who ever might need
to sit and rest our heads
and in the bright light
open our eyes.

In Paris, with you

the trees are different here

the sky is different

and your face
is the same

like how the sun is
and the moon too

even if each night
a little bit of it goes away   the moon
and each of the other nights it gets a bit bigger

so also I suppose
my heart too
like the moon

a little bit littler
on some nights
and some nights
a bit bigger becoming
shifting its weight
depending on the light
but still
under the darkness
it is the same moon
always round
and full

like too the sun

even as the sun hides
here in the trees
of Luxembourg Gardens

or is caught rather
between the snares of their branches

as we sit under them
in this summer hour
many summers away

from the April
where I first saw you
in a different country than this one
with different trees
with a different sky

and with your face

like the moon
    the sun
      my heart

    the same

Chalcedony

Do you remember when
after we had been eating chicken and rice
and I said to you that I always love you
but today, right now,
I'm in love with you?
And you smiled sheepishly
and sweetly and at the same time
and I said to you
that your face looked like an ocean agate, glowing.
Do you remember this?
Surely, my love you must. It was just last week.
And it was such a very sweet thing for me to have said to you.
And such a sweet way for you to have made me feel.
So sweet I had to write it down. Here.
For you. For me. For us both.

Hurt II.

Often when I think about your face I hurt in my body
can feel it in my belly behind my cheeks like a mountain ready
to canyon and the only way I cannot collapse all of me from out of me
is by just hurting this dull ache like a stone-shaped shape in my gut—
it's like how sometimes it hurts to look up at the night sky and see it
somehow looking up at me still with all of us inside the sky too or how
sometimes the only way to show certain music that you love it is by trying
to shake your bones out of their skin or how sometimes when a piece of
delicious food tastes so good all you can do is scream it is like this—I just
want to scream but I have roommates and it is late and my throat ain't
what it once was so I won't bellow at least not now not right now instead
I'll just lay here in my bed two hundred miles away from you with a
mountain between me and that mouth of yours that holds those two lips
I love and simply hurt cuz of the iceberg machine of your eyes first Xerox
of the stars glowing and unnamed fruit grown from out the aurora of
Georgia that beautiful fucking dance of light and song long eyelashes and
like the softest cheekboned peach that is your face.

Somewhere in the Bend

Over the mountain I drove, to see her for her birthday, and through some snow. I do not miss departures, do not miss a driving away from. I do miss arriving, whether those I love have reached my doorstep or I have gotten to theirs. It is such a sweetness, to travel to each other's homes and to be, upon arriving, let inside. We drove farther, to sit in the hot springs. In Riley, we passed the tiniest post office painted the palest green sitting in the middle of a snowy nowhere, like the softest patch of grass. We went through snow-dressed desert and under sunny skies and towards mountains blue in the going and purple in the return and up hazy fogged curves and past winter-coated towers and into Burns and out of Burns with thin ice on the streets melting under the day and stared at the tundra become mist become flakes become field become flakes of snow again, and got out of the car and crunched over the white crunch and dressed down to walk the cold in bathing suits and down jackets and stepped into hot hot water to celebrate her thirty-ninth, and my book got wet, and that's okay because I got to read it anyway while water of the planet held me like a tub, and with the steam coming off the surface and the moon watching while hiding somewhere inside the day's wide and eastern light, I put her long arms over my shoulders and she wrapped underwater her knees around my hips and then between her legs slid her suit to the side to slip me inside of her and there we were moving and barely while smiling at one another like both of us were the same secret spoken in the sky's ear like the moon at two p.m., before we got out and dried off under the cold air and drove back west with that secret moon being now so full and glowing that somewhere after Riley and before Bend we had to pull over to see the naked fullness better and finish what we had started back at the springs under the eyes of the sun letting the shine of the now moon do what it does when it sees being done what it wants to do with a body of another, for it too is a body being bathed in and with the light of another one, arriving and aching to come inside.

To the sea

Sometimes when you start to ramble
or rather when you feel you are starting to ramble
you will say *Well, now I'm rambling*
though I don't think you ever are.
And if you ever are, I don't really care.
And not just because I, and everyone really,
at times fall into our own unspooling
—which really I think is a beautiful softness
of being human, trying to show someone else
the color of all our threads, wanting another to know
everything in us we are trying to show them—
but in the specific,
in the specific of you
here in this car that you are driving
and in which next to you I am sitting beside
with regards to you
and your specific mouth
parting to give way
to the specific sweetness that is
the water of your voice
tumbling forth—like I said
I don't ever really mind
how much more
you might keep speaking
as it simply means
I get to hear you
speak for longer.
What was a stream
now a river.

Marseille I. August's end

Arrived from Paris by train. Upon our arrival and unsure what food was open for us, we followed our hunger. We walked to see the sea. Walking down street-wide outside stairwells and up the steps of alleys thin as creeks. Flowering vines over the pale walls leaked in bunches like the lavender I smelled alone in Oxford years back. I was hungry then too. A different hungry, and a similar hunger. The first store we walked to was closing, for good. We took again to the alleys of light. Found a bakery, handful of ham croissants. Took them to the street's end, where the edgeless sea was across the traffic lights, below the stone walkway. Sat and ate while watching the blue and green Mediterranean, watched its bright rippling stretch into light. So blue, so green. So both full and empty. The distant rocks. Being kissed by the water without sound. We wolfed the croissants down and wanted more. Too hungry to talk even our own tongue much less French, still being understood by the woman who knew English and hunger and so smiled sincerely in telling us the pizza she could make for us. Like babies we nodded happily. Afterwards gelato and afterwards a want for more gelato, and a wanting to only eat gelato the whole time, but only having it once. Something about the city my mother loves, it feels like Italy even with me having never been. Here, everything becomes a painting. Walking down flights of stairs to swim in a pool hidden by jungled trees. Feeling alone. Feeling far from home. Feeling full. Feeling tides. Understanding my mother more now for her longing of Southern France. Wondering what other aches in her have called from past branches, what thick figs she longed to reach for but were not the ones on the tree for her to eat. Never tiring of what the hour was doing to the plump body of the sky, the ways it would blush above us. Everything is a song. Everything here is a song. You. Coming out the night sea to press your mouth to mine. We walked there from where we slept, under a blueing to indigo night and orange lights and cliffs with houses hovering over us and the cars and down the stairs to the inlet and swim out into this sea, your lips tasting of salt, the two of us, full, and still so hungry. A song I tell you. I can hear it still, even now with all this country laying between then and here and you and me. A song I hear. You and me.

In summer

I was loved.
I loved.

And the hours
were filled

even when
they were empty

with golden light.

And again

in summer
I was loved
again

and the hours then
again even when
they were empty

with golden light
were filled.

And again I was loved

and in summer.
And again
and again

filled and empty
and again.
With golden light
I loved and am
loved and again
and again I
love
again
and again
and again again.

Acknowledgments

The poem "There was a house" takes as its jump off the line "Spent nights last sleeping like two fours" from the song "Tiderays" by Volcano Choir.

The poem, "Translation of a song from somewhere else I do not remember" came from Spanish lyrics of a song I do not know, that was posted on Instagram by Anna Fusco, aka @lordcowboy. The lyrics that were shared, I ran through Google translate, and feeling something in me spark a little, continued running the words through a number of differing languages, before building a poem from these.

Some of the poems in this collection first appeared in some form or another in these publications or on their websites, for which I am so very grateful:
Academy of American Poets
Pigeon Pages
Midst
Green Mountains Review
Bitter Southerner

Some poems of people I love and cherish very much did not find their way into this book, or possibly yet out of my heart and on to the page. A poem for Cristin O'Keefe Aptowicz, about the love I needed my last year living in Austin, Texas, and of which she had to give me; a poem about my niece and my nephews, and my struggle to know how to make known to them my love for them, both through the pandemic's distance and the distance of my own self; a poem that mentions my sister and my brother; multiple ones about my parents; a poem yet unwritten about Derrick Brown and the two of us getting to live together for a few weeks in January 2022 in Tigard, Oregon, as we balmed our bruised hearts and wrote poems under the same roof, and in the mornings he would sometimes knock on my door with a smoothie he had made for me; as well as multiple poems for multiple people whom I have loved and been loved by over the past several years.

About the Author

Anis Mojgani is a writer and artist from New Orleans. The author of six books of poetry, an opera libretto, and a picture book, Anis lives in Portland, Oregon, where he serves as the state's tenth Poet Laureate.

www.thepianofarm.com

If you like Anis Mojgani, Anis likes...

How to Love the Empty Air
Cristin O'Keefe Aptowicz

Amulet
Jason Bayani

No Matter the Wreckage
Sarah Kay

Love Ends in a Tandem Kayak
Derrick C. Brown

Write Bloody Publishing distributes and promotes great books of poetry every year. We are an independent press dedicated to quality literature and book design.

Our employees are authors and artists so we call ourselves a family. Our design team comes from all over America: modern painters, photographers, and rock album designers create book covers we're proud to be judged by.

We are grassroots, D.I.Y., bootstrap believers. Pull up a good book and join the family. Support independent authors, artists, and presses.

Want to know more about Write Bloody books, authors, and events?

Join our mailing list at

www. writebloody.com

Write Bloody Books

After the Witch Hunt — Megan Falley

Aim for the Head: An Anthology of Zombie Poetry — Rob Sturma, Editor

Allow The Light: The Lost Poems of Jack McCarthy — Jessica Lohafer, Editor

Amulet — Jason Bayani

Any Psalm You Want — Khary Jackson

Atrophy — Jackson Burgess

Birthday Girl with Possum — Brendan Constantine

The Bones Below — Sierra DeMulder

Born in the Year of the Butterfly Knife — Derrick C. Brown

Bouquet of Red Flags — Taylor Mali

Bring Down the Chandeliers — Tara Hardy

Ceremony for the Choking Ghost — Karen Finneyfrock

A Constellation of Half-Lives — Seema Reza

Counting Descent — Clint Smith

Courage: Daring Poems for Gutsy Girls — Karen Finneyfrock, Mindy Nettifee, & Rachel McKibbens, Editors

Cut to Bloom — Noah Arhm Choi

Dear Future Boyfriend — Cristin O'Keefe Aptowicz

Do Not Bring Him Water — Caitlin Scarano

Don't Smell the Floss — Matty Byloos

Drive Here and Devastate Me — Megan Falley

Drunks and Other Poems of Recovery — Jack McCarthy

The Elephant Engine High Dive Revival — Derrick C. Brown, Editor

Every Little Vanishing — Sheleen McElhinney

Everyone I Love Is a Stranger to Someone — Annelyse Gelman

Everything Is Everything — Cristin O'Keefe Aptowicz

Favorite Daughter — Nancy Huang

The Feather Room — Anis Mojgani

Floating, Brilliant, Gone — Franny Choi

Glitter in the Blood: A Poet's Manifesto for Better, Braver Writing — Mindy Nettifee

Gold That Frames the Mirror — Brandon Melendez
The Heart of a Comet — Pages D. Matam
Heavy Lead Birdsong — Ryler Dustin
Hello. It Doesn't Matter. — Derrick C. Brown
Help in the Dark Season — Jacqueline Suskin
Hot Teen Slut — Cristin O'Keefe Aptowicz
How the Body Works the Dark — Derrick C. Brown
How to Love the Empty Air — Cristin O'Keefe Aptowicz
I Love Science! — Shanny Jean Maney
I Love You Is Back — Derrick C. Brown
The Importance of Being Ernest — Ernest Cline
The Incredible Sestina Anthology — Daniel Nester, Editor
In Search of Midnight — Mike McGee
In the Pockets of Small Gods — Anis Mojgani
Junkyard Ghost Revival — Derrick C. Brown, Editor
Kissing Oscar Wilde — Jade Sylvan
The Last American Valentine — Derrick C. Brown, Editor
The Last Time as We Are — Taylor Mali
Learn Then Burn — Tim Stafford & Derrick C. Brown, Editors
Learn Then Burn Teacher's Guide — Tim Stafford & Molly Meacham, Editors
Learn Then Burn 2: This Time It's Personal — Tim Stafford, Editor
Lessons on Being Tenderheaded — Janae Johnson
Love in a Time of Robot Apocalypse — David Perez
The Madness Vase — Andrea Gibson
Multiverse: An Anthology of Superhero Poetry of Superhuman Proportions — Rob Sturma & Ryk McIntyre, Editors
My, My, My, My, My — Tara Hardy
The New Clean — Jon Sands
New Shoes on a Dead Horse — Sierra DeMulder
No Matter the Wreckage — Sarah Kay
Oh God Get Out Get Out — Bill Moran
Oh, Terrible Youth — Cristin O'Keefe Aptowicz

1,000 Black Umbrellas — Daniel McGinn
Open Your Mouth like a Bell — Mindy Nettifee
Ordinary Cruelty — Amber Flame
Our Poison Horse — Derrick C. Brown
Over the Anvil We Stretch — Anis Mojgani
Pansy — Andrea Gibson
Pecking Order — Nicole Homer
The Pocketknife Bible — Anis Mojgani
Pole Dancing to Gospel Hymns — Andrea Gibson
Racing Hummingbirds — Jeanann Verlee
Reasons to Leave the Slaughter — Ben Clark
Redhead and the Slaughter King — Megan Falley
Rise of the Trust Fall — Mindy Nettifee
Said the Manic to the Muse — Jeanann Verlee
Scandalabra — Derrick C. Brown
Slow Dance with Sasquatch — Jeremy Radin
The Smell of Good Mud — Lauren Zuniga
Some of the Children Were Listening — Lauren Sanderson
Songs from Under the River — Anis Mojgani
Strange Light — Derrick C. Brown
38 Bar Blues — C.R. Avery
This Way to the Sugar — Hieu Minh Nguyen
Time Bomb Snooze Alarm — Bucky Sinister
Uh-Oh — Derrick C. Brown
Uncontrolled Experiments in Freedom — Brian S. Ellis
The Undisputed Greatest Writer of All Time — Beau Sia
The Way We Move Through Water — Lino Anunciacion
We Will Be Shelter — Andrea Gibson, Editor
What Learning Leaves — Taylor Mali
What the Night Demands — Miles Walser
Working Class Represent — Cristin O'Keefe Aptowicz
Workin' Mime to Five — Dick Richards

Write About an Empty Birdcage — Elaina Ellis
Yarmulkes & Fitted Caps — Aaron Levy Samuels
The Year of No Mistakes — Cristin O'Keefe Aptowicz
Yesterday Won't Goodbye — Brian S. Ellis

Printed in the USA
CPSIA information can be obtained
at www.ICGtesting.com
JSHW082148140823
46539JS00002B/15